Sun Signs: The Stars in Your Life

by

Amy Shapiro

A
cpi
Book

From

RAINTREE CHILDRENS BOOKS
Milwaukee • Toronto • Melbourne • London

Copyright © 1977 by Contemporary Perspectives, Inc. All rights reserved. No part of this book may be reproduced or utilized in any form or by any means, electronic or mechanical, including photocopying, recording, or by any information storage and retrieval system, without permission in writing from the Distributor and the Publisher. Inquiries should be addressed to the DISTRIBUTOR: Raintree Publishers Limited, 205 West Highland Avenue, Milwaukee, Wisconsin 53203 and the PUBLISHER: Contemporary Perspectives, Inc., Suite 6A, 230 East 48th Street, New York, New York 10017.

Library of Congress Number: 77-21393

Art and Photo Credits

Cover illustration by Lynn Sweat.
Illustrations on pages 4, 10, 11, 14, 15, 16, 21, 25, 28, 31, 33, 37, 40, 42, 44, 45, and 48, Mary Kornblum.
Photos on pages 7, 18, 24, 35, and 46, Wide World Photos, Inc.
Photo on page 26, Culver Pictures, Inc.
Photo on page 38, "The News."
All photo research for this book was provided by Sherry Olan.
Every effort has been made to trace the ownership of all copyrighted material in this book and to obtain permission for its use.

Library of Congress Cataloging in Publication Data

> Shapiro, Amy, 1943-
>   Sun signs: the stars in your life
>   SUMMARY: A short history of the development of astrology, a brief explanation of how the planets supposedly control our lives, and a discussion of the personality traits for the different signs of the zodiac.
>   1. Astrology—Juvenile literature. [1. Astrology] I. Title.
> BF1708.1.S5   133.5   77-21393
> ISBN 0-8172-1028-8 lib. bdg.

Manufactured in the United States of America.
ISBN 0-8172-1028-8

Contents

Chapter 1
Sun Signs—Calm, Cool, Confident Scorpio 5

Chapter 2
Sun Signs—Sense or Nonsense? 11

Chapter 3
Sun Signs—Aries, Taurus 18

Chapter 4
Sun Signs—Cancer, Leo, Virgo 26

Chapter 5
Sun Signs—Libra, Sagittarius, Capricorn 34

Chapter 6
Sun Signs—Aquarius, Pisces, Gemini 43

Sun Signs—the symbols of the zodiac—*top*: phases of the moon, *outer wheel*: names of sun signs, *middle wheel*: animal or object symbols of the stars, *inner wheel*: astrologer's shorthand symbols for sun signs.

Chapter 1

Sun Signs
Calm, Cool, Confident Scorpio

The football game was almost over. Fifteen seconds remained. The score pretty much told the story of the hard-fought game. It was 7-6 and the small crowd was starting to walk away from the little Long Beach, California park. *"A good game." "Too bad for the losing team." "Nothing they can do to win at this point."*

The "losers" were little more than halfway down the field. They had the ball, but time was against them. "Time out," called the captain, a tall thin boy who wanted to win this game. He looked to the sideline. Was there anybody on the team who could help? His eyes moved from face to face. Scott? Ricki? Moffitt? *Moffitt!* Billie Moffitt just might save the day! But how could he explain this to the other guys?

Billie Moffitt put on a helmet and scrambled onto the field. A field goal would have to be kicked more than 50 yards! Billie was good, but that was a long way to kick the ball. Well, no one could ever accuse Billie Moffitt of not trying. Billie was a shy kid with a reputation for being "cool under fire." Close friends knew, however,

5

of Billie's fierce desire to win and strong drive to be, not just good, but *the best* on the field.

The center snapped the ball and placed it end down in time for Billie's kick. The kick was hard and the ball left the grass with stunning force. It moved in a perfect arc towards the distant goal posts. Billie, along with every boy on the field, stared at the ball's flight. Was it powerful enough? Was it high enough?

The kick was perfect! The ball sailed through the goal posts. As soon as it hit the ground, boys seemed to run from every direction to where Billie stood. Who ever heard of such a thing? This kid just won a game that was all but hopeless! The score was 9-7 and the "losers" *won.*

One of the boys pulled Billie's helmet off. Four more picked Billie up on their shoulders. The fans and the boys on the other team could only stand, mouths open in amazement, as the winners carried their idol off the field. Without a helmet Billie's hair had fallen down to the top of the numbers on her football jersey. For the first time the other team realized they had just been beaten by a *girl.*

Billie Moffitt is a grown woman now. She is still a great athlete and she still hears the cheers of the crowd. Her game has changed and so has her name. Today, she is known as Billie Jean King, queen of professional tennis. But very little else about Billie Jean's personality has changed from the time she was born.

Billie Jean King was born on November 22, 1943. In the language of astrology, that means she was born under the sun sign of *Scorpio*. The sun was in a zone of the heavens that astrologers have named Scorpio. Ancient people drew pictures of the stars in Scorpio that looked like the scorpion (a poisonous spider) and the eagle. Following is what an astrologer would tell you about a Scorpio. See how closely it fits the Billie Jean King you know. For that matter, see how well it fits anyone you know who was born on or between October 24 and November 22.

Scorpio (The Scorpion/The Eagle)
October 24 through November 22
Your element is water
Your ruling planets are Mars and Pluto

In talking about people born under the sun sign of Scorpio, and for all the other sun signs in this book, we describe four different features:

- *the animals most like the ancient sun sign drawings* (the spider and the eagle)

- *the birth dates that fall under the sun sign* (October 24 through November 22)

- *one of the four elements* (as the astrologer, not the scientist, would use the word) *that most influences these sun sign people* (air, fire, earth, or water)

- *the planets that most affect the mind, personality, speech, movement, and emotions of people under the sun sign, depending upon where the planet was in the sky when they were born* (for example, Scorpios born when Pluto was in another sun sign may also behave like people in that other sun sign)

A Scorpio is usually a person in pretty good control of things. Calm, clear thinkers, Scorpios appear calm and quiet on the outside. But inside there may be a lot more going on. Scorpios want to *win* at what they do or play. They can be angry and determined even when they look most relaxed.

The Scorpio is self-assured in work and play. Tell Scorpios they are talented and they very well might answer, "I know." Their will to win and their quiet confidence, combined with generally powerful bodies, help make Scorpios good athletes.

Little seems to bother or frighten Scorpios. They seldom tell others when they are hurt or in pain. But while they keep their own feelings locked away carefully, they can pull out of others their most hidden secrets.

Scorpio is surely one of the most powerful sun signs. Remember the ancient symbols for Scorpio? While the scorpion can sting, the eagle can soar to any height. More U. S. presidents have been Scorpios than any other sun sign.

Some Famous Scorpios

Marie Antoinette	Billy Graham
Richard Burton	Katharine Hepburn
Daniel Boone	Grace Kelly
Dick Cavett	Robert Kennedy
Johnny Carson	Billie Jean King
Prince Charles	Pablo Picasso
Nadia Comaneci	Theodore Roosevelt
Chiang Kai-shek	Jonas Salk
Madame Curie	Rock Hudson

Scorpio—Winter people, Scorpio's are *cool*. They are calm, clear thinkers—quiet outside but boiling inside.

Chapter 2

Sun Signs
Sense or Nonsense?

What do *Harry Houdini, Thomas Jefferson, Charlie Chaplin,* and *Diana Ross* all have in common? How about *Sigmund Freud, Willie Mays, Ulysses S. Grant, Socrates,* and *Barbra Streisand?* How are they alike?

They are all famous people, but they seem to have little in common. Yet there are some who would say that they are more alike than you would think. These famous people are bound together by their *sun signs.* So are you and all the other people who share your sun sign. That's just what this book is about. *Astrologers* believe that people's lives are mainly guided by the sun's position in the heavens on the day and at the very moment they were born. An astrologer claims to know a great deal about you, even without meeting you, just from your birth date.

Here are the names of the sun signs and the birth dates that come under each. Find your own sign and the signs of your friends and family. Then read on.

If your birthday is on or between	*Your sun sign is*	*Your star picture is*
Mar. 21 and Apr. 20	ARIES	the Ram
Apr. 21 and May 21	TAURUS	the Bull
May 22 and Jun. 21	GEMINI	the Twins
Jun. 22 and Jul. 23	CANCER	the Crab
Jul. 24 and Aug. 23	LEO	the Lion
Aug. 24 and Sept. 23	VIRGO	the Virgin
Sept. 24 and Oct. 23	LIBRA	the Scales
Oct. 24 and Nov. 22	SCORPIO	the Scorpion
Nov. 23 and Dec. 21	SAGITTARIUS	the Archer
Dec. 22 and Jan. 20	CAPRICORN	the Goat
Jan. 21 and Feb. 19	AQUARIUS	the Water Bearer
Feb. 20 and Mar. 20	PISCES	the Fish

Later, while you read about your sun signs, it's important to remember that, to astrologers, your sun sign is the main influence on your personality. But it is not the only influence. The moon and your planets are important, too. You may even be guided by more than one sign. This often happens if you were born at the very beginning or at the very end of a sign. Astrologers refer to this as being born on the *cusp.*

Billie Jean King was born on November 22, the end of Scorpio. She may, therefore, have some Sagittarius qualities because it is the sign just after Scorpio. To be absolutely sure Ms. King was born a Scorpio you would have to know the exact time of her birth. Then you would need to find out whether or not the sun had already left Scorpio to enter Sagittarius by that time of day.

Astrology is anything but new. The ancient astrologers believed that the sun and moon were the most powerful gods in the sky. They ruled over the gods of earth, fire, air (wind), and water.

These astrologers thought that the planets were powerful, too, so they named them after their gods—Mercury, Venus, Mars, Saturn, and

JUPITER

MERCURY

MARS

SATURN

The planets were named for the powerful gods.

14

Jupiter. From the tops of their temples, they mapped the heavens. They noticed the planets because they seemed to move around the sky more freely than the stars.

The ancient astrologers followed the path of the planets through the sky. The planets passed 12 sets of stars, or *constellations*. The ancients called this path the *zodiac*, a Greek word meaning "animals." The stars in the constellations outlined the shapes of different animals. Each constellation was named for the animal shape it formed. One looked like a bull. It was called *Taurus*, a Latin word for bull. Another, resembling a fish, was named *Pisces*, and so on. Each of these 12 constellations became a *sun sign*.

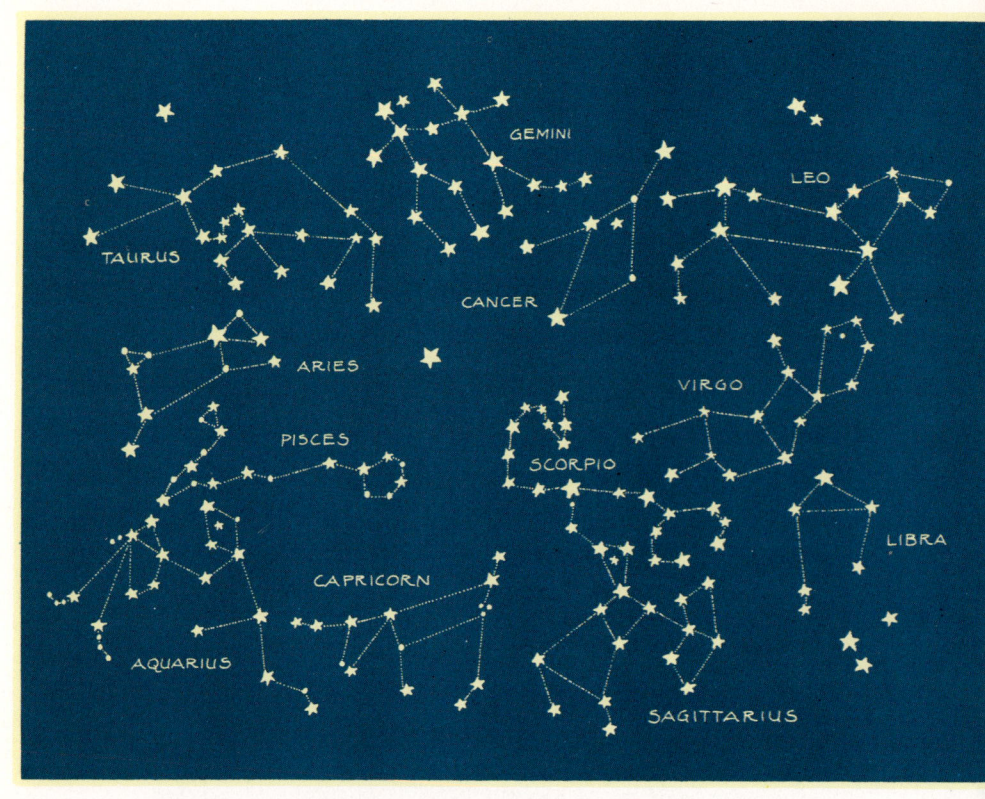

The constellations are "star pictures" within the zodiac—an imaginary area of the heavens.

Today, astrology is practiced all over the world. In fact, there are some people who will not make any important decision without checking their daily *horoscope,* a chart that shows the positions of the heavenly bodies. Astrology is so popular that almost every newspaper features daily horoscopes. And some people even have their own astrologers.

Astrologers believe that at the very moment you were born, the positions of each star and planet helped create a special you. By knowing the exact time and day of your birth, an astrologer can chart the positions of these heavenly bodies. This information, say astrologers, helps you understand where you are heading and why.

At the same time, many other people believe that astrology is nonsense. We are what we are, they say, because of what we inherit from our parents and what we receive from the world around us. The sun, the other stars, the moon, and the planets in the heavens have nothing to do with the kinds of people we are or become.

Before *you* draw any conclusions about whether or not astrology is a science, read on. Do you fit the description of your sign? Do your friends? Does your family? To help you get started, we have supplied some stories about famous people who seem to match their sun signs, according to astrologers. In Chapter 1, we used Billie Jean King, whose personality and special abilities seem to perfectly match what astrologers say Scorpios are like.

Every time you find a perfect match, however, remember that the nonbelievers can always find a person who doesn't seem to match his or her sun sign at all!

Chapter 3

Sun Signs
Aries, Taurus

The newspapers had just hit the street when President Thomas Jefferson's office door flew open. A young assistant, cheeks flushed with excitement, almost fell over his own feet as he rushed into the room. "Excuse me, Mr. President . . . for not knocking, I mean. I had to show you this!" In his hand he waved the afternoon newspaper. "It's treason, sir, that's what it is! There should be laws keeping the newspaper people from printing such lies!"

Startled, President Jefferson took the newspaper. He motioned for the excited young man to sit down opposite him. As the President read the front page, a look of sadness showed clearly in his eyes. The angry news story said President Jefferson was allowing his hatred for his former Vice President, Aaron Burr, to overcome justice. Burr was on trial for treason against the United States of America.

"No matter what you do in life, son," said the President, "you can't get everyone to like you. The newspapers have a right to their views and I will defend that right to my death." Jefferson was true to his word. No matter how awful the stories about him in the newspapers, he defended his "free press" ideals every day of his life.

Thomas Jefferson was born April 13, 1743, under the sign of *Aries*—the Ram. He was a good student, a musician, and an athlete. Most of all, Jefferson had a lively imagination. The combination of intelligence and imagination led to a part of his life few people knew about. Thomas Jefferson was an inventor—a *good* one. Jefferson was also a lawyer and an accomplished architect (he designed *Monticello* himself).

Thomas Jefferson was a great national leader and a man who seemed to be interested in *ev-*

erything. He studied foreign languages and the languages of the American Indians, and he built a collection of over 10,000 books in a lifetime of reading.

Aries (The Ram)
March 21 through April 20
Your element is fire
Your ruling planet is Mars

People born under Aries, the first sign of the zodiac, are fun-loving, natural leaders. Aries people love to be adored. And when they're not, "rams" get very hurt. Nobody can ignore Aries children, and the word "no" never stops them! It doesn't even work when they're older because Aries people need something or someone to fight for. Give them a dare or a challenge and zoom! Off they go! "Rams" can butt their way through any problem and come out on top.

Aries people are very affectionate and generous and usually have many friends. Their terrific imaginations lead to new inventions and many bright ideas. But watch out! "Rams" often begin lots of new projects before completing those they have already started. But an Aries will defend an ideal to the "bitter end."

Aries—A springtime sun sign. These affectionate, generous people are natural *leaders*. Aries people are imaginative and make good sales people and politicians.

Because they're such good leaders, "rams" can run almost any business they find challenging. They also make good salespeople or politicians because they get along so well with others. Some Aries people enjoy painting, music, writing—anything that requires a vivid imagination.

Some Famous Aries

Marlon Brando	Harry Houdini
David Cassidy	Thomas Jefferson
Hans Christian Anderson	Eugene McCarthy Wayne Newton
Charlie Chaplin	Diana Ross
Julie Christie	Arturo Toscanini
Bette Davis	Vincent Van Gogh
Aretha Franklin	Tennessee Williams

The date was April 24, 1942. Within the universe the tiniest fragment of history was being made—the earth people were involved in a world war. A bigger event was taking place within the solar system. The sun had entered Taurus, and in less than a month it would enter Gemini. And if the war raging on earth was a tiny fragment of history, what can we call the birth of one baby girl in a New York hospital?

The young girl grew up in a part of Brooklyn called *Flatbush*. She was far from the prettiest girl in her school—Erasmus High School—and she certainly would never win any popularity contests. Her teachers say she was a fair student but one who was stubborn and had a fierce temper. When she didn't want to do something, it was hard, if not impossible, to get her to do it. Normally quiet, she would flare up if she felt forced to do something she disliked.

But while single-mindedness was a problem in school, it may have been the young girl's most helpful quality later on in life. She had a wonderful singing voice, and she knew it. By her late teens, she was sure that she wanted a singing career. Her mother, stepfather, and older brother tried to convince her that a singing career would be impossible. The family didn't have enough money for voice lessons and professional training. She would have to get a "real" job to support herself and give up the idea of singing.

Today, she still has a temper. She is still stubborn. She is also one of the brightest stars in show business. She has entertained millions of people around the world in plays, movies, and on records. Always concerned with money as a child, she has earned millions of dollars as one of the highest paid performers of our time. The name of the young *Taurus* from Brooklyn is *Barbra Streisand!*

**Taurus (The Bull)
April 21 through May 21
Your element is earth
Your ruling planet is Venus**

Taureans are as stubborn as bulls. They are easygoing people most of the time—that is, until they don't want to do something. Then they just don't do it! On the other hand, when a Taurean *wants* to do something, it gets done no matter how long it takes.

"Bulls" are very practical and love to earn money. They almost never spend their earnings foolishly. And they're the most likely candidates for class treasurer. Not surprisingly, many bankers are born under this sign. So are many millionaires!

Taureans are very serious and hate to be teased. They can be pushed just so far. Then they can become violent. Danger: Watch out for "the bull."

Some Famous Taureans

Johannes Brahms	Willie Mays
Glen Campbell	William Shakespeare
Salvador Dali	Socrates
Ella Fitzgerald	Barbra Streisand
Sigmund Freud	Shirley Temple
Ulysses S. Grant	

Taurus—These springtime sun people are easygoing, but watch out—they can be stubborn, too. Practical and "stick-to-the-job" types, they earn and save money well. Chances are this boy is earning money taking care of a neighbor's plants.

Chapter 4

Sun Signs
Cancer, Leo, Virgo

There was an air of sadness and fear throughout the castle. The year was 1542 and Henry VIII, King of England, had ordered the execution of his fifth wife, Catherine Howard. She was the second to be beheaded by order of the restless and violent King. Never content with anything for too long, Henry VIII let nothing stop him from snatching each new thing he wanted.

Under the reign of Henry VIII, England had thrown off the religious rule of the Roman Catholic Pope. The King became the head of his own new religion—the Church of England. He did away with wife after wife—there were six of them before he died—and beheaded every advisor who had suggested his brides to him. Now, he had grown tired of Catherine. The King, born to the sign of *Cancer*—the crab—would bring the blade of the ax to rest at the under side of his fifth wife's lovely neck.

King Henry VIII, the "fitful King of England," would marry once more. His sixth wife was another woman named Catherine. There might have been a seventh wife, but, luckily for wife number six, the changeable King died.

Cancer (The Crab)
June 22 through July 23
Your element is water
Your ruling planet is the Moon

Cancer, the fourth sign of the zodiac, is ruled by the ever-changing moon. Because of this, Cancerians are moody, quiet, and sensitive. Even as children, they change constantly, giggling at one moment, flooding the room with tears at the next. They need constant love and approval from their family and close friends.

People born under the sign of Cancer are often "crab-like" in the way they attack problems.

Cancer—A summer sun sign of the moody, quiet people ruled by the moon.

Once a goal is set, Cancerians will go from side to side, getting nearer to the goal. Then, just as someone else goes after the same thing, Cancerians grab for it, holding on tight and never letting go.

Cancerians are often shy and keep to themselves. Others may share their secrets with them, but they keep their feelings inside. At the same time, once a Cancerian trusts and likes you, you've got a friend for life. If hurt, a Cancerian is too proud to admit it. And the "crab" remembers every feeling and experience.

Cancerians can be by themselves for hours. As children, many of them have imaginary friends and spend hours lost in daydreams. Cancerians seem especially "tuned in" to other people. They often seem to know things even before they're told!

Some Famous Cancerians	
P. T. Barnum	Henry VIII
Julius Caesar	Mick Jagger
Calvin Coolidge	Helen Keller
Phyllis Diller	Rose Kennedy
John Glenn	Rembrandt
Susan Hayward	Nelson Rockefeller
Ernest Hemingway	Red Skelton

Leo (The Lion)
July 24 through August 23
Your element is fire
Your ruling planet is the Sun

Leo, the lion, is the king of the zodiac. Leo people are brave, energetic, and commanding.

Leos must always be leaders. It is not part of their nature to take second place, and they'll let you know it in no uncertain terms. Leos are organizers who can tell others what to do. They prefer the important jobs, letting less powerful workers tackle the small details. But Leos beware: It's hard for you to turn down any responsibility. You sometimes bite off more than you can chew.

Leos are outgoing, friendly, and often have big, warm hearts. Their many friends know that they can count on them in any emergency. The lion feels responsible for the weak. And although at times a Leo may be frightened, he or she will still be a powerful opponent when defending those cared about.

Leo—Summer people who are organizers—born leaders. Ambitious and energetic, Leos are ideal for acting and show business careers.

Some Famous Leos

Neil Armstrong
Lucille Ball
Bill "Count" Basie
Napoleon Bonaparte
Fidel Castro
Julia Child
Cecil B. De Mille
Henry Ford

Alfred Hitchcock
Herbert Hoover
Jacqueline Onassis
Princess Margaret
George Bernard Shaw
Andy Warhol
Mae West

Virgo (The Virgin)
August 24 through September 23
Your element is earth
Your ruling planet is Mercury

Virgos, those born under the sign of the "virgin," are considered very practical and down to earth people. Their lives must be neat and orderly. Even as babies, their food must be prepared just as they like it.

If a Virgo finds fault with someone, he or she can be very harsh. As for their own shortcomings, no one knows these better than the Virgo.

When others shy away from hard work and duties in school, the teacher can always call on a Virgo. People under this sign can handle a lot of hard work and responsibility. And they see to each and every detail carefully and, much of the time, perfectly. Virgos take things very seriously and rarely make mistakes.

Virgos are private people. Crowds make them uncomfortable and nervous. So even though they're good in school, Virgos have a hard time getting up in front of the class to recite.

Some Famous Virgos

Lauren Bacall
Ingrid Bergman
Leonard Bernstein
Sid Caesar
Henry Ford II
Buddy Hackett
Jesse James
Lyndon B. Johnson
Joseph Kennedy

Lafayette
D. H. Lawrence
Sophia Loren
Queen Elizabeth I
Peter Sellers
William H. Taft
Roy Wilkins
Hank Williams

Virgo—People born under this summer sign are practical, down to earth, and very hard-working. Serious and dependable, Virgos do better when they are away from crowds.

33

Chapter 5

Sun Signs
Libra, Sagittarius, Capricorn

The young naval officer peered out into the night. Standing on the bridge of his submarine, he watched the last patches of moonlight disappear from the sky. Soon there was only the inky darkness and the swelling of ocean waves. A storm was approaching and the young officer was beginning to feel a bit sick as the submarine tossed and rolled in the choppy sea.

As the storm built, waves began to wash across the submarine. Fear made its way into the young man's mind as he awaited the order to come below. He was sure the "skipper" would take the boat below the water and wait out the storm. Right now, however, he had a station to guard and he was holding tight to the metal rail in front of him just to stay on his feet. Suddenly a mountain of water charged over the bridge. When the water settled down again, the submarine bridge was empty!

No one below deck had heard a thing. The officer thrashed about in the water, trying to swim back to the boat through the churning sea. It was rough going. It seemed that for every foot he swam, the driving waves would push him back two. But he finally rose high on a giant ocean swell and, as the water fell back, found himself clinging to a forward gun. He was back on the boat *and he planned to stay there!*

The young navy officer, known as an intelligent, gentle man, hardly surprised his friends as he smilingly told them what had just happened. His fellow officers had grown used to his quiet, cheerful manner in the face of even those jobs he hated the most. The sailors also knew him to be an intelligent, able officer who always listened to every side of an argument. He reached a decision slowly, but in just about every case his decision was a fair one.

The young navy man born under the sign of *Libra* would, within the next 30 years, go on to become the Governor of his home state of Georgia and the President of the United States. His name is Jimmy Carter, and he won what may be the greatest political upset in history.

Libra (The Scales)
September 24 through October 23
Your element is air
Your ruling planet is Venus

Libra's symbol, the "scales," tells a lot about the personalities of people born under the sign. Libras must balance everything in their lives. Sometimes the scales move up and down before reaching an even balance, and this may make it difficult for a Libra to make a decision.

If you've ever seen someone try to break up a heated argument and smooth things over between two angry people, chances are that person was a Libra. They try to be fair and just with everyone, constantly working for perfect harmony.

Venus has a strong influence on Libras' love of the arts. But anything loud or harsh to the eye and ear annoys Libras. They love soft music and classical art, and many are probably very artistic themselves.

Some Famous Librans

Brigitte Bardot	F. Scott Fitzgerald	Arthur Miller
Sarah Bernhardt	Mahatma Gandhi	Eugene O'Neill
Chuck Berry	George Gershwin	Pelé (Edson Arentes
Jimmy Carter	Le Roi Jones	do Nascimento)
Dwight D.	John Lennon	Eleanor Roosevelt
Eisenhower	Franz Liszt	Paul Simon

Libra—A fall sun sign. *Artistic* people live under this sign—people who are fair-minded and balanced. Look for Libras to "patch up" arguments between others.

Uri Geller is thought by many people to be an amazing—perhaps *incredible*—young man. He is a *Sagittarian* who was born on December 20, 1946 in Tel Aviv, Israel. If you can believe what your eyes tell you when you watch him perform, Uri Geller bends metal objects *without ever touching them!* Among many other "magical" gifts, he appears to be able to stop and start clocks by simply looking at them.

Uri Geller has become the center of a worldwide mystery. There are people who believe that he has mental powers that allow him to read people's minds. These people believe he can "see through" sealed envelopes—even concrete walls—and make objects move without touching them. But many more people believe he is simply doing tricks that other magicians do on the stage. People who know Uri Geller say that he performs in theaters because he loves the attention of people.

Uri Geller appears to be a cheerful, well-liked person. Only when he is challenged by magicians to confess that he is only doing stage tricks does he become very angry. His bursts of bad temper are quickly over when people surround him and begin asking him questions about himself. At this point, Uri often gets himself into some trouble with his stories. He has been known to mix up details of his life and say things about himself that are just a little different than what he has told others just a few hours before.

All who have seen Uri perform agree on one point. No one in the crowd loves what Uri does more than Uri himself. When a key bends or a broken clock starts, he gets as excited as a little boy. "See," he says, "I told you! I told you I could do it!"

Sagittarius (The Archer)
November 23 through December 21
Your element is fire
Your ruling planet is Jupiter

While Sagittarians can recall almost every conversation they've ever had, they can forget details and where they put things. They like to take part in team sports but may fumble the ball every now and then. And they have good senses of humor—but often mix up the punch lines of their jokes!

Sagittarians love and need to be around people. They love to talk to everyone they meet, sharing ideas and being the center of the action.

Sagittarius—A sign of the late fall, Sagittarius people love crowds. At their best when they are the center of attention, they are talkative, sharing people.

Their constant curiosity makes "why?" one of their favorite words. And their many interests and love of learning make them good students. On the other hand, Sagittarians may lose interest if they're bored or the routine becomes rigid.

Some Famous Sagittarians

Louisa May Alcott	Noel Coward	Ira Gershwin
Ludwig van Beethoven	Sammy Davis, Jr.	Frank Sinatra
	Joe DiMaggio	David Susskind
Billy the Kid	Walt Disney	Mark Twain
Winston Churchill	Dick Van Dyke	Uri Geller

Capricorn (The Goat)
December 22 through January 20
Your element is earth
Your ruling planet is Saturn

If you're a *Capricorn*, you're probably as sure-footed and independent as your symbol, the goat. You strive to reach the top, overcoming any obstacle in the way.

Capricorns have a very practical nature and watch everything very closely. They tend to plan things out, step by step. And sometimes they worry about the next step before they're finished with the one before it. Capricorns are natural leaders. They love to take on responsibilities. They do well in school because they're good organizers. Capricorns are ambitious. They love hard work and challenge.

When it comes to being with people, Capricorns prefer a small group of truly loyal companions to a great many casual friends. They keep to themselves much of the time, too.

Some Famous Capricorns

Steve Allen	Cary Grant	Mao Tse-tung
Humphrey Bogart	J. Edgar Hoover	Mohammed Ali
Pablo Casals	Howard Hughes	Richard Nixon
Nat "King" Cole	Danny Kaye	Elvis Presley
Benjamin Franklin	Martin Luther King	Helena Rubinstein

Capricorn—Winter people, sure footed and independent as a mountain goat. A very practical people, planners and organized, ambitious leaders.

Chapter 6

Sun Signs
Aquarius, Pisces, Gemini

Aquarius (The Water Bearer)
January 21 through February 19
Your element is air
Your ruling planets are Uranus and Saturn

Aquarius is the water-bearer, pouring out his life force (water) to the whole world. An Aquarian is concerned with kindness, honesty, and equality for all people. In fact, astrologers consider Aquarius close to being the most perfect sign of all.

Aquarians have a thirst for learning all they can about everyone and everything. They love to read and probably have more books than games. Think of the people who get the answers to problems more quickly than anyone else. They're probably Aquarians. Their teachers may wonder how these bright-eyed Aquarians get the answers so fast—especially because Aquarians seem to be in a dream world most of the time!

Aquarius usually has lots of friends. Giving undivided attention to each person, he or she can find out other people's deepest feelings and everything there is to know about them.

Aquarius—A winter sign: To astrologers, Aquarians are the "perfect people." They look to books for knowledge. They are dreamers and yet they are problem solvers. Highly popular, they give their attention to everyone.

Some Famous Aquarians

Tallulah Bankhead	Charles Dickens	Abraham Lincoln
John Barrymore	Jimmy Durante	Charles Lindbergh
Jack Benny	Thomas Edison	Leontyne Price
Lewis Carroll	Mia Farrow	Franklin Delano
Charles Darwin	Clark Gable	Roosevelt

Pisces (The Fish)
February 20 through March 20
Your element is water
Your ruling planets are Jupiter and Neptune

Pisces is pictured as two fishes, one swimming upstream, the other swimming down. And like this symbol, people born under Pisces can either strive upwards with great hope for the future or, when things look bad and the stream of life is not going right, they can easily give up.

Pisceans are great charmers who easily win people over. It's a good thing—because they also need a lot of love and reassurance. Pisceans don't have a great deal of confidence in themselves. And they are very sensitive, the kind of people who cry easily.

It is very hard for a Piscean to follow a schedule or routine. Pisces infants often get their days and nights reversed. When they want to sleep, they sleep, and when they're hungry, they have to be fed—no matter what time of day it is. Later on, these children find it difficult to follow a schedule in school.

Pisces—These late winter people are *sensitive*. They cry, even give up easily. Pisces people need a great deal of love.

Some Famous Pisceans		
Edward Albee	Jackie Gleason	Dinah Shore
Harry Belafonte	Rex Harrison	Svetlana Stalin
Elizabeth Browning	Ted Kennedy	John Steinbeck
Enrico Caruso	Michelangelo	Elizabeth Taylor
Frederic Chopin	Rudolf Nureyev	Earl Warren
Albert Einstein	Auguste Renoir	George Washington

Born May 29, 1917, John F. Kennedy, thirty-sixth President of the United States, was a son of *Gemini*. His public life is known the world over, as are the stories of his heroic deeds as a torpedo boat commander in World War II.

Young John Kennedy was a fiercely competitive athlete. At Harvard College he was a fine swimmer and football player. A strong and constant reader, Kennedy was graduated from Harvard in 1940 with high honors. After war broke out in 1941, he tried to enlist in the army. He was refused because of a back problem he had ever since a college football injury. After a year of exercise to strengthen his back, he was accepted by the navy.

While commanding a PT boat in the Pacific in 1943, his craft was rammed by a Japanese destroyer. Although his back was hurt again, young John Kennedy towed one of his men to safety. Kennedy swam through five miles of ocean, clenching the wounded sailor's life jacket in his teeth.

What is less well known about John Kennedy is that he won a Pulitzer Prize in 1957 for writing a book called *Profiles In Courage.*

Gemini (The Twins)
May 22 through June 21
Your element is air
Your ruling planet is Mercury

Gemini is one of the few signs that doesn't stand for an animal. It's the sign of the twins. And that's what Geminis often are—two people rolled into one! At one moment a Gemini might be extremely happy. Yet at the next moment he or she may be sad. But Geminis are not unhappy for too long. They are always able to find some new activity to pick up their spirits.

Gemini people are usually swift of body and mind. Their quick minds usually make them the

Gemini—A spring sign, the sign of the twins. Good speakers and writers, Gemini people are quick in mind and body.

first to read. As they continue school, Geminis are good speakers. They also like to write. You'll probably find a few of these "twins" reporting for the school newspaper.

Gemini—fast thinking, changeable, quick to act, imaginative, and usually the life the party!

Some Famous Geminis

Judy Garland	Tom Jones	Cole Porter
Paul Gauguin	John F. Kennedy	Igor Stravinsky
Bob Hope	Paul McCartney	John Wayne
Burl Ives	Marilyn Monroe	Walt Whitman